Then,

Something

Then,

Something

Patricia Fargnoli

Poems **Patricia Fargnoli**

T|P

TUPELO PRESS

North Adams, Massachusetts

Then, Something
Copyright 2009 Patricia Fargnoli. All rights reserved.
ISBN 978-1-932195-79-8

COVER AND TEXT DESIGNED BY HOWARD KLEIN.
Cover photograph by Brian Jecker. Used with permission.

Excerpt from "For Once, Then, Something" from *The Poetry of Robert Frost*, edited by Edward Connery Lathem.
Copyright 1923, 1969 by Henry Holt and Company. Copyright 1951 by Robert Frost. Reprinted by
permission of Henry Holt and Company, LLC.

First paperback edition September, 2009.
13 12 11 10 09   5 4 3 2 1
Printed in Canada.

Fargnoli, Patricia.
Then, something/Patricia Fargnoli.—1st paperback ed.
p. cm.
Summary: "A septuagenarian poet nearing the climax of life explores boundaries between nature and human,
body and spirit, faith and skepticism, and real and imaginary"
—Provided by publisher.

ISBN 978-1-932195-79-8 (pbk. : alk. paper)
I. Title.
PS3556.A7144T47 2009
811'.54-dc22

2009016775

Tupelo Press
P.O. Box 1767, North Adams, Massachusetts 01247
Telephone: (413) 664-9611 / Fax: (413) 664-9711
editor@tupelopress.org / www.tupelopress.org

Tupelo Press is an award-winning independent literary press that publishes fine fiction, non-fiction, and poetry
in books that are a joy to hold as well as read. Tupelo Press is a registered 501(c)3 non-profit organization, and
we rely on public support to carry out our mission of publishing extraordinary work that may be outside the
realm of the large commercial publishers. Financial donations are welcome and are tax deductible.

NATIONAL
ENDOWMENT   Supported in part by an award from the National Endowment for the Arts.
FOR THE ARTS

for Alycia, Joe, Joshua, and Jessica

Contents

IV.

V.

Once, when trying with chin against a well-curb,
I discerned, as I thought, beyond the picture,
Through the picture, a something white, uncertain,
Something more of the depths—and then I lost it.

Robert Frost, from "For Once, Then, Something"

I

Wherever you are going

You will want to take with you the mud-rich scent breaking through March frost
  and lemons sliced on a blue plate, their pinwheels of light.

You will want to take strawberries you have stolen from the farmer's night fields
  and the sleepy child you lifted from under the willow where she'd been playing.

You will want to take the one-eyed horse that was never yours and the obstinate cat that was
  and the turtle with the cracked shell you found crossing the hard road and could not save.

You will want, especially, to bring with you the shifting blue/black/grays of the lake shining
  beneath coins of silver and all that lives deeper there beneath the mysteries of water.

You will try to take a prayer you might have otherwise left behind in case you need it—
  and a memory of the love you have been calling back—but you will soon forget.

When you go, you will leave the Giants cap you wore to dinner behind for the others,
  you will leave dust coating the books you meant to read, the books themselves

weighing down the shelves. It will be necessary to leave the suitcases and tote bag
  in the overcrowded closet and your two rooms for someone who wants them

more than you ever did. Leave your tickets and your Master Charge with its sad balance—
  you won't be coming back regardless of what you've always been told. Therefore take nothing,

take less than nothing and even less than that. Remove your shoes, place your pulse on the table,
  release breath, leave behind the scars on your finger, your thigh, the long one over your heart.

On the Question of the Soul

It is not iron, nor does it have anything to do
with the fleshy heart. It does not shiver

like feathers nor the arrow shot from the hunter's bow,
is not the deer that runs or falls in the snow.

It hunkers down in the invisible recesses
of the body—its closets, scrolled bureaus,
the ivory hardness of the chest,

or disperses through every cell. And also it flies
out beyond the body.

Someday watch smoke travel through the air.
Someday watch a stain spread out to no stain
in the ocean. The soul does that.

It doesn't care whether or not you believe in it.
It is unassailable and contradictory: the dog
that comes barking and wagging its tail.

It is not, I am certain, biology.
Not a cardinal or a heron, not even a thrush or wren,
but it might be a praying mantis.

It is the no color of rain
as it sweeps a field on an August morning
full of fences and wildflowers.

It is the shifting of light across the surface
of any lake, the shadows that move like muskrats
across a mountain whose shape mimics the clouds above.

Weighed down by the vested interests
of the body, it nevertheless bears us forward.

The Phenomenology of Garbage

She is sitting there watching the garbage man
who pulled in as she was about to back out,
his green and white truck
blocking her way, so there's nothing to do
but watch as he climbs down from the cab
and goes around to the barn to haul out barrels.
Because every moment's
an occasion for attention
she notices the name, *Cheshire Sanitation*,
and it makes her wonder what's being sanitized,
certainly not yesterday's turkey
along with the *Boston Globe*
and a popped volley ball
cranked down into the dark dragon maw
and smashed into some essence
of turkey/ball/*Globe*,
that makes her think of Zen,
how everything's connected.
And not the truck which smells like rotten pears,
and not the barrels, filthy, but emptied out
for now of what she doesn't want—
the unendable excess.
And because she can't go anywhere,
she sits there (in her Toyota Corolla
with the rusty gash on its side)
as the grind
of the compactor drowns out
her dog singing in the barn, nose in the air,
and she wonders where all this stuff is going—
(not only to the dump, which is obvious)

but in the long run—
matter, not able to be created or destroyed—
the atoms of some long-gone Magna Carta
perhaps even now storming around in her blood,
kicking up her irritable bowel
or hurtling this precise minute
in the leftover turkey leg bone
down into the compactor—
Being brought forward
all the way from the Big Bang,
the whole mess collapsing
to no-time and all-time
the way everything's a paradox,
like her thoughts which are going
everywhere and nowhere ...
which are at a dead end
and no end (so to speak), blocked
by this metal Magog rumbling before her.

Almost Ghazal with Thoughts Toward Spring

Nothing loosens the way a brook loosens from April,
ice hurls up along the edges, block after giant block.

Peepers rev up, mole salamanders breed in vernal pools.
It seems as if the voices of the song birds all unlock.

A poet I knew lived in a mountain cave, wrote on trees
and sang to the wind. Light's time, his only clock.

Animals have souls also, and trees and blossoms, maybe rain.
Once, I thought I saw a soul embedded in a rock.

The dream world is another as real as this. I pass between the two,
as through a membrane, through a line, or arc.

Winter leaves me in a hush, trailing its long scarf of hours. What door
slides back at last, Patricia? Light comes in. No need to knock.

Applewood Senior Apartments, April Again

You'd been told it would come to this, the turning away
into smaller and smaller rooms. The footsteps upstairs
are not anymore a husband's, but the thin neighbor
      who comes and goes beyond your window,
his sick cat in a carrier.

Across the way, an old woman tends the peonies
of an old man, their lives not even connected to yours,
but other somehow—a kind of out there—
      as if you were watching
the reel of your own past life passing.

Once, you had a life and it was sometimes good.
Your hair was auburn then, you could run.
If only your legs would move today in that remembered
      ease and rhythm.

Once, you could escape time in the arms of the man you loved
on Sunday afternoons in a rooming house with faded walls,
      drawn shades and a green light bulb.

Spring's long past due, snow sheeting down again. On the walks
the maintenance man spreads his icy poultice of salt.

Late Snow

The light's unbearable.
      What was frozen melts again—

the waterfall of water falls and falls.
      This late snow's been nothing but a lamb

upon whose woolly head Spring breaks
      into the broken world, o bright, o bright.

The Cows of Walpole, New Hampshire

A dozen gathered near the gate, lying down,
backs touching, chewing side to side.
The air was full of rain not yet falling, a slight rancid
pungency of cows, the vegetation of full spring—
all its weedy green and field flower.

The Guernsey lying nearest poked her heavy sculpture
of a head through the bottom rail and side-glanced at me,
her white-lashed eye pink-rimmed as an old woman's eye,
pale blue as bleached denim.
I reached out to pat the grimy curls plastered along her nose.

She shied her head away but quickly turned back to allow my hand.
Respectful of her need for distance, I monitored my own,
but took in the mud on boney haunches, hooves,
bone-hard, large as twice my fist, the whole herd's expirations:
snuffs and snorts that resolved into steady quiet breathing.

Theirs was a mild curiosity, they looked at me then looked away.
Perhaps I was the day's entertainment—an aging woman,
a strange being stalled at their boundary.
I wanted to enter their world and told them so
in what I hoped was something akin to their language.

I said I was tired of my own, and went to lie down
among them through those overcast hours toward the end of May
when I was heavy with too much solitude.
It began to rain the finest mist-rain, and I lay there a long time
breathing in the rhythm of their breathing.

Easter Morning

Gray and cold, Christ rises again—or not.
Suits and lilies in the churches
where organ music ascends to wherever it goes.
The old woman in the upstairs apartment
has gone out garbed in red, her white hair neat
above her rounded back.
I am alone in here, as if waiting
with unbelief and belief.
Overnight the heat
has dropped too low. I turn it up.
Later, I'll go for lamb shank and sherry
with a neighbor. Lately, I've been worried
about death, how it will come too soon.
Part of me wants release
but we cling to life, most of us,
with passion—or not.
Hung in my window, a hummingbird,
blue and red stained glass, drinks
from a white flower. Life,
we sip at its nectar.
Yesterday, after my reading,
a man handed me two paragraphs
about his shaky spirituality, saying
mine had helped with his own,
and a widow my age claimed I'd changed her life.
Such praise, hard to let in, harder to let go.
What do they know
of me except what I've written?
And what has that to do with this
awkward woman fiddling with her fingers,

biting skin off her lips,
becoming reluctantly old?
I live slowly these days,
puddled, stagnant, longing for rest, but wanting
ridiculously to be a hero, a Gandhi
leading crowds in my long white robe.
A weather vane spins on the cupola
of the building across the way. It's the ordinary kind—
brass letters for the four winds, topped with a rooster.
An arrow points to all the directions
on this earth it is possible to be given.

II

Pemaquid Variations

New Harbor, Maine September 8–15, 2001

I.

Tonight, on its surface, the ocean harbors
      twelve thousand stars. The sand is the sea's brother.
Sky opens out beyond my greed to understand it, and I
      am alone here, wandering across the beach,
carrying a scavenged branch as walking stick to scratch my name.

II.

Stones' weight in my pockets, driftwood,
      a worm-pitted scrap, gull-feather dried, hollowed
light as wind. Here, beside this unnamed
      crescent beach the ocean's tamed to bay.
Waves, small, hurl their tidy spray across the dark,
      their gravely soft-talk, strange repetons,
no less intelligible to their own kin, I think,
      than my inadequate speaking is to mine.

III.

This place is respite; this place is compensation
      for what cannot be wholly compensated.
The terrors permeate my skin
      which is too thin to resist them:
blood murders war and war and war,
      griefs that worm their way into my spirit.

I run from what I cannot bear into my many
        busy dances. But here night blinds me—
I cannot see the waves, the world's all sound,
the lulling tongues, over and over
        taking away the shore, and leaving
wrack and kelp and mussels, their blue brokenness.

IV.

Night weighs the stones and makes the sea.
Night, the thief that climbs the ladder to your child's room.
Night is the comforter the mother has thrown across the waves.
Night howls at a distance in the hills from the dry dens.
Night is pitted with wormholes and stars.
Night is more than we can imagine and less than God.

V. *Song for two voices*

Come lover, let us dance together down the dark sand
        Come lover let us dance
  I will not dance with you, I love another
     I will not dance
    Through the marsh path, down the dark beach come
     I am no lover of yours   *I will not dance*
    Come lover let us dance
       no, I love another
        down the dark beach let's dance.

VI. *For three overlapping voices*

Night, *the weigher of stones*
         the maker of the sea.
                  Night, the weigher of stones

Night, *more than we can imagine*
         the maker of the sea
                the weigher of stones.

and less than God.
        Night, *more than we can imagine*
          the maker of the sea

and less than God.
        Night—*more than we can imagine.*
         And less than God.

VII.

On the day after the hurricane,
when the rain had stopped pounding
the cliff by the lighthouse,
I saw three old women in lawn chairs
pulled near the edge as if theirs were
the best seats at a hit play.
They were watching the ocean
shatter great waves against the cliff.
Each new wave its own performance.
Over and over the hurled water rose
thirty feet in the air and smacked
the stone with a beastly roar,
spume flying up to the cliff-top.
Each time, the women shouted and clapped their hands.

VIII. *For three children, voices overlapping*

the children are running on the beach in the sun
    the children are running on the beach in the sun
        the children are running on the beach in the sun

the mother is tanning her skin by the shore
    the mother is tanning her skin on the shore
        the mother is tanning her skin on the shore

the father is absent, he's shipped out to war
    the father is absence, he's shipped out to war
        the father is absent he's shipped out to war

IX. *Credo*

Tonight, to believe in God seems impossible. Only the mythology
    we recite against the dark. I am walking alone
on the beach at the mouth of the bay.
    September, the sand cool beneath my bare feet.
I have chosen to walk in darkness in order to take in
    what I cannot see—the small mouthings
of the waves as they roll across the tideline stones
    and retreat again,
the comforting predictability of their rhythm,
    and the night air full of salt and the scent
of barnacle-crusted wrack left hours earlier by the high tide,
    the musty-ripe smells of the marsh
beyond the row of scrub pines. If there were a moon
    it would lay a trail across the darkness, but there is no moon,
only a faint phosphorescence on the waves—
    a magic that illumines nothing of importance.
Even the stars have retreated behind a spread of high clouds.

X.

In the night, after the hours of unquiet sea,
out of New Harbor the storm passed.
We tired of days of the grayness pressing down
and went out in the sun.
The villagers came to the beach with balls and dogs
and the children with tin pails and much shouting.
They ran here and to, on the sand.
A hubbub of voices, the business
that put the storm in the past. Twelve thousand
spoons danced on the wave tops—a vast glittering.
By twilight, the blues, a large school of them,
had made their way in close to shore, and the gulls,
knowing this, lined up facing the sea, and the fathers knew
the time was right and came down on the beach
and cast their lines into the water
and pulled fish one after the other,
and piled them in silvery piles on the sand.
They threw back all except the largest,
as the sun went down in a splash of glory
that lit the waves with a shimmering gold/bronze/vermillion light.

XI.

When the news came, we were stunned
and could not believe this had happened.
When the news came.

We were stunned, we sat like stones
in the beach cottage, before the televisions,
and could not believe.

This could never happen,
Then the news came.

In the cottage, before the televisions,
we sat like stones.

XII. *poeta fui e canai di quel Giusto**

What is our fault in this, the terror that descended into the middle
of our complacency? To suggest that we have fault
is not to say others are blameless. But that mussels
tempered by the sea are broken on the shore.

XIII. *Nocturne*

soft soft   soft soft now
the combers come in
and the moon's bin of platinum
pours over the bay
and the hard sand beneath me
walking at tideline
and the sound of the water
sweet life-filled saltwater
where the sea weeds are drifting
rocking and rocking the night
wraps around me,
close as a blanket but
stretching to everywhere and
soft   soft   soft   soft
          the waves
come *in in in in*

XIV. *Retardando*

Stones' weight in my pockets, driftwood,
a worm-pitted scrap, gull-feather dried, hollowed
light as wind. Here, beside this unnamed
crescent beach the ocean's tamed to bay.
Waves, small, hurl their tidy spray across the dark,
their gravely soft-talk, strange repetons,
no less intelligible to their own kin, I think,
than my inadequate speaking is to mine.

XV. *Return*

Tonight, on its surface, the ocean harbors
twelve thousand stars. The sand is the sea's brother.
Sky opens out beyond my greed to understand it, and I
am alone here, wandering across the beach,
carrying a scavenged branch as walking stick to scratch my name.

* *Inferno*, Dante, Canto 1, l. 73: *I was a poet and I sang the righteous*

III

Alternate Worlds

They are what fuels the dark, what lies
beyond the sheer curtains.
They are mysterious and hooded
like the woman in your dream, the hollow
before birth, what hides beneath the casket lid.

And this also: what whoops out
from the forest, the claws
of moles in their tunnels, the moon's
long fingers trailing across cheekbones,
the breath dispersed into ether.

You can see them from the corner of your eye,
hear them hum in the background of everything.
Or, on a summer night, a huge moth,
white-winged, full of grace,
darts across your path—and is gone.

Pastoral

There are so many messages I can't interpret.
The hundred maples at the edge of my street shout orange, orange, orange,
in silent voices. And may say more if I could decipher.

How I want to understand the many calls of the birds migrating through
on their long journey. And what is the message of the shaggy
wave-curled sea quarreling around the black rocks out at the far point?

Perhaps words themselves wander off into other fields, like sheep lost
in the depths of the hills beyond the local hills so the shepherd has to go climbing
up and down, his legs aching, his breath heavy in his chest until he spies them

off there under that far evergreen, and wrestles them down and brings them home.

Grackles

We had been walking too far for any hungry people,
       our hotel many blocks behind us.

Restaurant after crowded restaurant turned us away.
       From trees transformed into silhouettes by darkness

sounds came that couldn't be called music,
       sounds that seemed to be the shape of the trees themselves,

mechanical sounds like many metal discs clapping,
       an ear-splitting hubbub, a dissonant racket.

I was having a tough time of it. The year-long
       sprained ligament in my heel made each step painful.

When I hung back, no one noticed.
       The lights from the restaurants spilled into the streets

and from inside those crowded places
       came frenzied music and hoots of laughter.

Passing headlights, jazz and blues, the city
       rumbling around me, that strange wreck of music in the trees.

I didn't want to go on. I wanted to lean against the trees,
       be taken in by the thousand rough avian voices.

The night roared with omen, some prophecy I alone
       was meant to receive.

Cold River Season

The river slid by in a mist like a mind unreeling
and clouds passed, thinning as they went.

Before the hour was over, they had disappeared.

Noon erased shadows from the banks
                and out of the woods two deer came,
carrying their vulnerable bodies with such dignity.

In the late afternoon, hunters came also,
death in their rifles.

We are like them, whether or not we want to be—
intense and after what we could leave alone.

As night approached, the river darkened—
                    wild silver to black.

The hunters strapped down their take, stashed their guns
in their pickups and vanished. The bottom stones also

              vanished beneath the current.
The oiled tarp of night covered everything.

The Parents

1942

He never showed up when he said he would—
          his absence a chime in a clock with no face.

Didn't she spend her life waiting
          by the Philco, by the black phone, for the letters
            that came scrawled darling and love.

Inside my shadowy memory of—
always his eyes. Darkened. Staring outward
          from the map of his world—

torn edges, sharp-peaked mountains and deep
          descents—some lost country of confusion.

Her skin grew pale then pallid until she seemed spectral.
She fell quiet as a pond when wind has died down
          and the water seems all reflection.

I don't remember her smiling—a constant sadness.
          What is lost?

She died young. He wasn't there.
          Some tavern in another state,
some glass of amber brandy kept him past the hour—

his spirit pinned to the odd calendar
          of a salesman's life.

From the beginning, she must have been fragile
as a glass bowl, delicate, etched with scrolls
                    and spirals that led nowhere.

A bowl that could hold her spirit even
                    as she lay dying. Holding and breaking

all at once—freeing her, I imagine,
                    into a land lovely as the tidal marsh
                    where one September, monarchs

weighed down each cluster of goldenrod
                    then lifted off—fragments of orange glass
                    glinting above the creek.

The Losing

The mother who left in my childhood
is leaving again in my dream.

She is leaving the ghost of a town
and has gone on to the next.

She has left the cottage door open,
the chair still rocking.

My mother is leaving again from the memory
of a white double bed,

her hands pale on the sheets, her face
pale as she leans against the headboard.

The child leans against the doorjamb,
crying because her mother is crying.

Something unbidden has entered the room,
something terribly wrong in the room's raw light.

There are two brown suitcases on the floor.
In the other room, two aunts wait on the sofa.

My mother left all my days and nights
and went into the illness for which

there was, in those days, no cure
and no slowing it down.

My mother escaped from my drunken father,
she escaped from the last days of the war,

she escaped from the snow that, in that last winter,
fell endlessly and everywhere.

In the field of my mother's absence,
two blackbirds are flying through the wind-driven snow.

Imaginary Sister

Beyond the front door, partly closed
      against dog days' heat, night was dropping down fast.

Smell of grass, newly mown, wet from the sprinklers.
      The children were still jumping rope at the corner.

I heard their chants, a scatter of gravel, and the mothers
      calling calling.

At the table in the other room, my sister was playing a game
      from the storeroom shelves.

She played alone whispering softly to herself
      as if someone was there. She was always sad

I remember, though her hair flared
      with the kind of moon-pale light that keeps

the darkness where it belongs. If only she'd answered
      when I called to her.

Instead, she drew away from me like a night-moth disappearing
      among the dark leaves of the magnolia tree.

Dante's Inferno

1961

I walked in to the blast of bump and grind.
A stripper in blue light was jiggling the yeasty dough
of her breasts in the face of a front-table guy.
He was there in back, clouded in cigar smoke,
just as I'd feared, drinking strega with five paisans.
Beneath my black maternity sweater our third child
thumped in my belly. He hadn't come home;
he never came home. It was 1 a.m. I was twenty-three.
I left the children sleeping. Left them!
I would have escaped if I'd known how—
no skills, no family, his dollars gone to ale,
the horses, Coronet Brandy.
Poverty. We lived it. The stove repossessed,
the cheap sectional worn through to foam.
More than forty years later I can barely say this.
He wouldn't leave the club. I begged him. He ignored me.
So I sat alone at an adjoining table
in the crowd of tables. Big Al and The Count
har-harring, as my husband, showing off, slid a dollar
from his suit pocket and lit it.
My eyes filled as the flame rose from his silver Ronson
to the bill, its fire curling
toward me, a tongue flicking, as if
the devil himself was teasing.
I breathed in its acridness, what could I do against this?
Nothing. I did nothing.
He's dead, the children near fifty. What stays?
That fire curling toward me, it still curls toward me.

I want to shriek at them: Chips, Big Red, Mike the Prince,
all of them, want to yank what is left
out of the burning air as if it is one dollar for milk,
one dollar for bread, one dollar toward rent,
one small necessary dollar.

In the dream, you grow long black hair, Herb

but that's not enough to save us, nor is the beam
we try to walk that runs six feet below the cathedral ceiling
of the apartment we've broken into—
spacious rooms that don't belong to me and never will.
I don't remember how we got up here, where we're suddenly
looking down on that couple cocktailing—
cheese and flatbread with their wine—on black leather couches,
in that space of chrome and glass that looks out over the city.
What *does* belong to me: the other apartment on a lower floor,

Uris #6, a shoebox cramped with red built-ins
I tried to tear apart with hate and my bare hands,
running from it finally to this forbidden living room.
When the beam breaks, dumping us into the couple's midst,
shattering their precious
glass, they call the cops and we take off
out of there, like some Bonnie and Clyde act,
veering down the hall and into an indoor flea market/carnival.
You are only words after all and I lose you

in crowded aisles with tables of bright secondhand clothes,
festooned lamps manned by men with hoop earrings,
men garbed in harem pants, blowsy purples, red silks.
I keep trying to turn invisible in the crush of revelers
but the cops, not fooled, continue their pursuit,
until, nowhere else to go, wiped out, breathless, I end up
back at the cramped apartment I've been trying like hell to escape.
And the inescapable cops are axing through the bolted door
I've thrown my entire weight against.

The Seduction

Somewhere in Europe, a city shines—torn tin, splintered glass,
bombed-out cathedral. Dangerous elevators fall forever.

So far, the young woman has survived. She rides the metro home.
Her dress, navy linen. Her hair, thin brown, pinned up.

The stranger beside her, staid, suit-rigid, pays no attention.
She presses against his shoulder, he shifts.

She leans again, lets flesh show, not much. Then a touch.
Accidental?

Between them a current—A palpable thing. Is this seduction?
Or something deeper?

Above the train, the blitz-scarred city. Around them,
the others blur. What she wants? For him to touch her too?

Maybe, but try again. What she wants: the solace of his body.
They are innocent, both of them.

The world speeds beyond the windows in constant flashes
of light and shadow.

The next day she waits. Will he come? No? Yes,
here he is. She lets her shirt fall away from her throat.

This move might save the fallen city, yes? no?
It's no surprise what will happen.

Fire

On this day there is a great fire,
the people gather all their belongings
and go out into their village streets and begin
to walk away into the countryside.
Smoke covers their past lives.
Ahead of them, the road is empty to the horizon.
In the fields, the sheep bow their heads to the grass
as if nothing is the matter.
The road is impossibly long, dirt, rutted, full of stones.
Nothing can be seen beyond the next mountain.
Eventually, the people get tired. Some fall
but the mass goes forward,
and some of the fallen stand again and struggle on.
I have to go down now
and mix in
and walk along with them.

IV

Old

After Po Chu-I's "Rain"

Since I lived an old woman at Applewood,
too many days the soughing ambulance sped in
and took away someone who wouldn't be back.

I had nothing to do but cook—and sleep many hours.

The dahlias are bending under the rain in the garden
beneath the windows, then the sun washes over them.

From the village, I hear car doors closing
and someone calling.

From a rooftop, I hear one mockingbird's many songs.

The yellow cat with closed eyes curls
around himself on his carpeted tower.

Blue rain, blue rain again, stipples the air conditioner.
Sun, rain. Rain, sun. Sleep. Sound. Watching.
Every day, these things occur, and nothing more.

A strange insect, long as my hand, black with pinchers,
clings to the screen.

Melancholy in Late October

Morning proffers rain. Around Dublin Lakes,
swamp maples try their last brilliant voices.
If there were no despair in me, I wouldn't know myself.

If I had been born blind, I might have known
the gift of impediment.
But I have my own handicaps,

skin so permeable as to be no boundary at all,
pain that comes the way a surgeon's knife
pierces the body.

The rowboats have been pulled from the water.
Soon, the lakes will be drained again,
leaving only mud beds

and the clocks will fall through the hour.
I listen to the chill wind
waiting to reclaim those I love.

In nearby fields, the horses are restless for winter,
the comforting dim light of barns.
Already the first flakes have fallen.

I have become extravagant—
I have turned on all the lamps in the house—
all day I keep them burning.

Pain's Song

You hear pain singing in the nerves of things; it is not a song.
　　　　　　　　　　　　　　　　　　　—Robert Hass

If it is not a song, then my sore body cannot croon itself to sleep,
nor sleep cast its long notes over the pond that drowns the moon.

If it is not a song, then why is it humming through my shoulders,
why do my legs thrum against the sheets?

If it is not a song, then what is it that carries its code
along the nerves to the concert hall my brain is,

its backstage rooms like those in a dream, one beyond the other,
all the connecting doors open to let the music through.

And what is the sexual song of the insects' last August days
and the weeping song of the woman raped in her narrow bed?

And what song did the bleeding boy sing from the street dirt?
Or the surgeon sing wielding his saw against a chest bone?

And if not song, then what is it the carved heart sings
to hold off death, its absence of music?

The Places Between

They are the spaces without words,
the warm snow underneath the cold
that stops the winterkill of roots,
the faint presence of burning
that hangs in the air before the fire
or the sound of birds whose songs
have been captured by wind.
They are the touch of no hand
when love has gone
or age has overtaken you,
the sight of a landscape
not yet seen, the length of rail
the train has not yet traveled.
They are the before and after,
the in-between, the last lilt
of the marketplace at dusk
when the vendors have rolled up
their squeaking awnings
in Haymarket Square, and Antonio
has shut himself behind his green door.
Because of the absent moments,
you will always be waiting
for something to arrive—
like Antonio
fresh from sleep, holding out
a round of goat's cheese
and a market-bag of yesterday's
peaches and plums.

Lullaby for the Woman Who Walks into the Sea

Poem beginning and ending with halves of a line by Ilhan Berk

Take your nakedness to the sea
and lie down at the tide line while the tide is still out.
Lie down at the wrack-ridge where sand pipers skitter
over dried seaweed, your whole body exposed that way,
your whole spirit exposed as you lie waiting.

With your whole spirit exposed as you lie waiting,
remember all that has passed that led to this place.
Remember the tall fields of childhood—
how you nested in the small circumferences your body
hollowed out in hip-high grasses, how the sun filled
the circle of sky you could see from that perspective.

Only the circle of sky you could see from that perspective
was contained enough to blanket you with its comfort.
Sometimes small quick swallows transected the wholeness,
their flights, diameters. Beneath you, the shaken universe
of the insects went on without your knowing. Out of your own
shaken world, Orphan, you had escaped to lie there

as in this shaken world you have escaped to lie here
naked and waiting at the perimeter of the sea,
for the tide that will, in only hours it seems,
return and wash over you, its watery brine a balm
on your face, its foam spreading under you,
lifting you like the mother you lost, her arms extended.

As it lifts you like a lost mother, your arms extended,
you will become a raft, bones rope-bound, wood buoyant,
and give in to the back and forth rolling of your own heartbeat
which keeps its watch over your body, which will become the sea,
which is, even now, beginning to be washed out, washed
into the waves and long sweep of wild waters.

Into the waves and the long sweep of wild waters,
you bequeath your grief, the many griefs that have entered your cells
and left their mark, the way algae clogging a pond surface
with its heavy green layer hides clear water. You bequeath the days
when your heart was a carousel of rise and fall.
You bequeath the reins. You let all you meant to control go.

The world you wanted to control and could not—you let it go
into the distances, into long sweep of wild waters.
You wait to be lifted by waves, mother-lightly, your arms extended,
away from the shaken world, Orphan, you have been wanting to escape,
all the sky you can see from that wide perspective will fall into the sea,
your whole spirit exposed as you lie here at tide line waiting—

willing your nakedness *to the darkening inswell of water.*

The Gifts of Linnaeus

After native New England plants named by Carl Linnaeus 1707–1778

What is sacrament if not to take in the names—
       the twinflower for instance he named for himself,
Linnaea Borealis, its fragile bells ringing

long past his brief moment in the world.
       Or smooth sumac for making ink, for spilling
on the page, for keeping what might be lost.

Not for me the altar rail or the intonations
       of the priest. Not the vessel lifted up,
nor the disk like a diatom on the tongue.

No, this is the body—this mountain laurel
       it is forbidden to pick, its blossoms like lights
against the dark woods, or the red mulberry

that failed to survive New England winters—
       someone's dream of silk that didn't come to pass.
And this is the body, the common milkweed's clouds

of blowing across the field, and this, too,
       what is left behind—the dried husk. And this
is the body—lobelia whose name fills my mouth.

And this is blood—the wild grapes clinging
       to the wall behind which the traffic
of the interstate rushes with a river sound—

and this too, high-bush blueberry whose bright
        gems gather a sheen of morning dew, their stain
on my willing tongue.

And here is New England aster, its flowers
        bluer than wine. Eat and drink: here, now,
on this giving earth, these sacraments.

Landscape in Black and White

We drive south from the White Mountains where wind
    bruises the treetops, dapples Echo Lake's surface,

drive through tundras of snow, our voices mingling
    over the motor hum.

Pristine towns pass with their steeples—white houses,
    closed gates. An old woman

tests a slippery walk with her cane. Her life's closing book of hours.
    Only night shines down on her.

Near White River Junction, smoke from the chimneys settles
    into snow banks. A freight train crosses a black trestle.

Around us, the season descends, we release our breath
    in a thin smoke to meet it.

Our words, sometimes caring, sometimes cruel, float through
    the closed car windows. Love, in my life you are everywhere.

Winter. This land, this time, this season. What music arrives
    we make with our own hesitant voices.

Winter Solo

traveling north from the sea
where cold water etches

black silt designs on the sand
   a woman drives through snow
   listening to someone far away

field   fence posts   the open gate
snow-flecks descending catch cabin light

an old man leans forward
   over an open book
his lamp shines down on it

moon's light travels as if
embedded in chords of music

arrives in my ear   the season
   is late descending
   my breath waits for it in dread

where are the wildflowers of August
and the silver-toned thrushes

song fluting through the ash trees?
   love   it has been many years
   you are no longer anywhere

on Black Lake a small rowboat drifts
far out   and how will it return

through water hardening to ice?
  scent of iron settles down
  on all objects nearby and far

summer   another land   time   season
a man and a woman meet in secret

under a salt tree   to love each other
  I tear the sheets from my body
  full of grief for what's been lost

Cows in Fog

A shroud covers the field and the hills behind it.

My eyes are white with loss

      in a landscape not meant for seeing.

The dampness permeates my skin.

      The distance rings with bells.

V

Then

Then, he held me there as if stunned, the figure who had appeared saying
    this is the edge between what is and what is not.

On one side was the forest in all its complex depth and verdancy,
    on the other side stretched the field, a wide field full of emptiness

where memory was hidden among the grasses, each day of the past moving
    like small winds there among the tall grasses.

And therefore I chose, leaving behind what was supposed to be left behind—

and grasped his luminous robe to follow, without a question,
    across the transition zone into the old-growth forest with its wing sounds.

I might have been the story that wasn't told—of the woman who left her home
    without looking back—changing forever what happened after.

I trusted only in that spectral figure who moved, with such grace, ahead of me
    into the dark evergreens, and the door of their branches closed behind us.

Meditation at Dublin Lake

The landscapes we know are not

   all the landscapes there are.

The spirit reaches after—

       there must be more

than this lake   its kaleidoscope of colors,

the monadnock that rises

already snow-topped beyond it.

Where is the being within and without

       over and under?

           How could we know?

Even that wood duck wings into a farther air

       and no matter what   I cannot follow

though sometimes I believe I can   and try.

I believe in the questions.

How many dancing universes?   And how far?

How small I am under them—
and yet …

Prepositions Toward a Definition of God

Beneath of course the sky,
in the sky itself,
over there among the beach plum hedges,

over the rain and the beyond and
beyond the beyond of,

under the suitcases of the heart,
from the back burners of the universe.

Here inside at the table, there outside the circus,
within the halls of absence,
across the hanging gardens of the wind,

between the marshland sedges, around the edges
of tall buildings going up
and short buildings coming down.

Of energy and intelligence,
of energy—and if not intelligence then what?

Ahead of the storm and the river, behind the storm and the river.
Prior to the beginning of dust, unto the end of fire.

Above the wheelbarrows and the chickens.
Underneath the fast heart of the sparrow,
on top of the slow heart of the ocean—

against the framework of all the holy books.
Despite the dogmas that rain down on the centuries.

Concerning the invisible and unnamable power,
in spite of the terror,

considering the spirit,
because of something in the body that wants to be lifted.

Because if not God, then what in place of

near the firebombed willow,
beneath the quilt that tosses the dead to the sky,

beside the still waters and the loud waters
and among the walking among?

Approaching Seventy

A spider crawls beneath the screen,
designs a web in the corner and waits
with the patience of a calendar.

This is the end of summer,
scent of decay everywhere in the outside air,

flowers, planted last spring with such
a sense of promise, leaving one by one,
disappearing into the earth.

I think of endings—

final page of a novel
and the characters you've come to love
placed on the shelf,

a wave from a doorway—those slight
or heavy sadnesses—

friend in Sagaponock the last time I saw her,
waving from the dock as the ferry pulled out
and the wake lengthened between us,

or swells on a stormy crossing,
pine boughs, dark, lifting and falling
in heavy rain, one night of my childhood,

beyond the small stair-top bedroom
at my aunt's Vermont inn, as I lay awake—
wood smoke and voices from the lobby below,

a memory of suitcases standing by a farmhouse
front door, milk cans topped with snow, the pale
complexion of my mother who left and didn't return,

memory of lilacs—branches my brother and I used to climb through,
scratching ourselves as we hid from each other—
not long ago, at an airport, we hugged goodbye again—

what I left behind when I moved
to this senior apartment—some feeling of usefulness,
half of my books, most of my clothes.

Sometimes, it feels as if I've said goodbye to everyone.
Through the north window, I watch clouds move off
beyond my vision and somewhere dissolve into rain.

Meditation in January

From my desk in this room,
only north light through two windows,

I watch the sky transmute, milky blue,
to the gray harbinger of more snow.

One crow traverses, heading I think for protection.
The wind picks up
and shivers through the sashes.

When did I begin to think of myself as old?

*

I fall back to a house ghostly in shape—
Around it, fields stretch to the tracks
and beyond to the river.

Ark of a house that is no more.
For years as a child I lived there and roamed those fields.

*

One day as the light was going, I went to the river,
the forbidden river. Bitter winter.
Ice like thinnest lace at the water's edge.

The snow which had started slowly to fall,
increased and swirled around me

hiding the lights of the house,
then hiding the whole landscape.
But I found my way.

That was the night a child I knew, a boy of seven,
tried a shortcut
to his home and froze under an oak.

*

Just before dawn the doorway
from my bedroom wears black.
The black is shadow night puts back
                              where light was.

The day is coming up gray beyond the pond,
rising out of night into the light-bloom.

The door to the room beyond this room—
what is, what thing is not quite real,
                              and waits there?

*

I am hoping for light—a death, easy as this memory:
a sun-blazed field,
Grand Isle on an August afternoon,

the deer stopped at the perimeter
between meadow and woods, reaching to pull down
leaves from the lowest branches into their tender mouths,

there where the sky is knitted to the field
their delicate bodies open to whatever comes.

*

But bless even the cold moments,
the snowstorm that fell last night
not with heaviness,
      but in the slantwise, wind-driven slurry
      that shifts and slides through day and into night
to fill the river with lessons about erasure,
      each thin flake dissolved into the whole.

Riddle

It is a tongue stud
that stumbles over its own words,
an ear ring that cannot hear,
a bumble on the nose of the flower.
It goes flying across the long field
that ends at a cliff beside the sea
that is rocking itself into shore
that is laden with shells, and stones
that knock against each other—
saying who knows what.
It's the Etoile
in Paris—tricky
to get on, hard to get off—
Mount Pilatus, its steep cog-rail
and dizzy ledges,
and it is the rug
I pull out from under you, both
the bird in the hand and the two in the bush,
the needle in the camel's eye,
the moat in my own, the dark glass.
It is a bridge
that crosses nothing
or the waterfall under it
tumbling into its own parameters.
Give it space
to breathe, scratch it
behind the ears, make it lie down
and be quiet, or rise
to the occasion, make it leap like
fire in the farm hearth—
then let it go.

After the Dream of My Death

I wake up to a world that is invisible,
no golden trees, no picnic spread on the lawn.
The ladies in hats have finished their tea
and moved on.

None of the questions I spent life asking
have been answered.
Transience, evanescence, the dispersal of dust.
God knows where, and is no where.

What good has my life been?
Whiteness sheets all that has vanished.
The hospital is gone. In the distance, a piano
casts its notes into the great absence,

which is where I've been heading—all along.

Metaphors from Late in Life

After Ilya Kaminsky

memory is an unopened closet stuffed with last year's undergarments
memory, a red ribbon, curls up under the knife of the present

*

love is the mouth and the cry that comes out of it, love goes running
like the thief the stranger chases through the city of loud pans

*

fear is the carnival after midnight when the lights flick out, fear,
the bandit, his knife, the one-armed ticket-taker at the freak show

*

pain is a ten times turned rack, pain, rabid beast's bite at your back
pain hooks sleep into its wild talons, and flies off with it

*

death is the short-order cook at the Sunset Restaurant
death, the chocolate maker who haunts your dreams

*

love is the chaos I run from, darkness makes me hide my head,
hunger is what drives me back into the world

Two Skeletons Found in a Barn Wall

One's arms around the other's middle,
delicate bones of the toes, the feet,
heads with their outsized eye sockets
in which I glimpse only shadow.

It must have been terrible, those last hours
in that darkest of places,
thirst setting in. Then hunger.
Only each other for companion.

Small inhabitants of this earth,
I don't know what I believe
or don't believe, but I wish for you
what I'd wish my own:

may you have found whatever solace
you needed from each other,
may you have found whatever heaven
is possible and awaits your kind.

Small Prayer Mosaic

the small prayer of the box

If I keep only darkness,
          you will need to search
for cracks, for seams,
for a door to open where there is no door,
          for light where there is no light.

the small prayer of the small voice

Where will my voice go if you leave me?
          When will you return? Within the next hour?
          Inside the letter? In spite of the rain?

the small prayer of the spoon

Lift me to your mouth that I may
          fill it with honey.

the small prayer of the cat

Let my talons be held withdrawn,
      my sharp teeth
          unneeded for this brief hour.

the small prayer of the door

Let me open, let them walk
          through me to the magic
          that is the garden.

Let them walk where all that has happened
                    can fall away and they can begin again.

the small prayer of the red-tailed hawk

Free of the earth and the hungers of the earth
                    let me spin above the fields,
let me rise in the thermals,
                    let me fall and rise, fall and rise.

Then, Something

The moose and his mate
                stood in the roadside marsh at dawn.
They moved the shallow sheet of water,
the smallest rustle,
                    as if ghosts were passing.

Together they broke the surface,
                such precision in their knobby bodies;
were they only figments in the unestablished light?
But something held them
                    bound them to the earth.

On a rise, above them, just at the edge of the road
                in a kind of trance,
I stood, leaning toward them, and for a long time
we stood in each other's company.
                    It was as if we were appearing

and disappearing in the dim light.
                The weight of shadow,
laden with gravity, shiftings, myths, a wild surrender.
We didn't move,
                    but might have been moving together

through the shallow satin of water,
                losing ourselves, it seemed, in truth and beauty.
Or am I only making something of them they were not?
Weren't they only two moose in a swale,
                pulling up water plants, chewing them

just before full day fell over the earth?

Coda

a woman walked away from the winter village,
became sand,
became ocean,
became sky.

Acknowledgments

Byline	"Riddle"
Cerise Press	"Alternate Worlds," "The Parents"
Cimarron Review	"Dante's Inferno"
Connecticut Review	"Two Skeletons Found in a Barn Wall"
Margie	"Easter Morning"
Massachusetts Review	"Prepositions Toward a Definition of God"
Mid-American Review	"Pemaquid Variations"
Nimrod	"Meditation in January," "Almost Ghazal with Thoughts Toward Spring," "The Gifts of Linnaeus"
Ploughshares	"Then"
Poetry International	"Old," "Fire"
Poetry Northwest	"The Phenomenology of Garbage"
The Poet's Touchstone	"Late Snow"
Valparaiso Poetry Review	"Cold River Season," "The Places Between"
Watershed	"Then, Something"

"Phenomenology of Garbage" was also published in the chapbook *Lives of Others* (Oyster River Press, 2001). "Prepositions Toward a Definition of God" was nominated for a Pushcart Prize.

My deepest thanks goes to my publisher Jeffrey Levine for his support of poetry and his faith in my work, and to Jim Schley for his careful editing and production management. Also to Mary Oliver for the many years and ways she's helped. I am grateful far more than it is possible to put into words for the encouragement and helpful suggestions of more friends than I can name here (and would be afraid to try, for fear of leaving out someone). But especially those in my workshops. A special thank you to Susan Roney-O'Brien, Lana Hechtman-Ayers and Ilya Kaminsky for their close reading and helpful comments on this manuscript, and to Herb Yood, Tim Mayo, Rick Bates, Pam Bernard, Shawn Supple, and Read Blinn for their long-term moral support. And to Roger and my family, who are my anchors to this earth.